THE STORY OF THE
MINNESOTA TIMBERWOLVES

THE NBA: A HISTORY OF HOOPS

THE STORY OF THE

MINNESOTA TIMBERWOLVES

NATE LeBOUTILLIER

CREATIVE EDUCATION

Published by Creative Education
P.O. Box 227, Mankato, Minnesota 56002
Creative Education is an imprint of The Creative Company
www.thecreativecompany.us

Design and production by Blue Design
Art direction by Rita Marshall
Printed in the United States of America

Photographs by Alamy (Scott Kemper), Corbis (ADAM
HUNGER/Reuters, CRAIG LASSIG/epa, ERIC MILLER/
Reuters, RAY STUBBLEBINE/Reuters), Getty Images
(Andrew D. Bernstein/NBAE, John Biever/Sports
Illustrated, Nathaniel S. Butler/NBAE, Jesse D. Garrabrant/
NBAE, Andy Hayt/NBAE, Frank Howard/Time & Life
Pictures, Glenn James/NBAE, Ken Levine/Allsport, Melissa
Majchrzak/NBAE, Manny Millan/Sports Illustrated, Joe
Murphy/NBAE, David Sherman/NBAE, Rocky Widner/
NBAE), Newscom (Marlin Levison)

Library of Congress Cataloging-in-Publication Data
LeBoutillier, Nate.
The story of the Minnesota Timberwolves / Nate
LeBoutillier.
p. cm. — (The NBA: a history of hoops)
Includes index.
Summary: An informative narration of the Minnesota
Timberwolves professional basketball team's history
from its 1989 founding to today, spotlighting memorable
players and reliving dramatic events.
ISBN 978-1-60818-438-5
1. Minnesota Timberwolves (Basketball team)—History—
Juvenile literature. I. Title.

GV885.52.M565L43 2014
796.323'6409776579—dc23   2013039307

CCSS: RI.5.1, 2, 3, 8; RH.6-8.4, 5, 7

First Edition
9 8 7 6 5 4 3 2 1

Cover: Forward Kevin Love
Page 2: Guard Ricky Rubio
Pages 4&5: Center Al Jefferson
Page 6: Guard Sam Cassell

TABLE OF CONTENTS

COURTSIDE STORIES

INTRODUCING…

A PERFECT PLACE FOR BASKETBALL

MINNEAPOLIS, MINNESOTA, AVERAGES THE COLDEST WINTERS OF ANY MAJOR U.S. CITY.

Minnesota's weather and the indoor sport of basketball is a match made in heaven. For each gust of icy wind, whirl of swirling snowflakes, and blast of freezing coldness, there is a toasty gym where none of that concerns anyone. On those warmly lit courts across the state, players while away the winter fully immersed in the glorious dribbling, passing, dunking, stealing, blocking, rebounding, and shooting—oh, yes, let us never forget the marvelous shooting—of the wonderful, scintillating, fantastical basketball.

It was in an environment much like Minnesota's—winter-chilly Springfield, Massachusetts—where the game of basketball was invented in 1891. And the game's inventor, Dr. James Naismith, perhaps unsurprisingly, hailed from similarly frigid surroundings in Almonte, Ontario, Canada, a small community on the opposite side of the Great Lakes as Minnesota. Professional basketball first came to Minnesota in 1947-48 when the Minneapolis Lakers joined the National Basketball League (NBL). The following season, the Lakers joined the Basketball Association of America (BAA) and took it by storm—or blizzard, you might say—finishing with a 44–16 regular-season record and winning the championship. For 1949-50, the Lakers joined the newly formed National Basketball Association (NBA) and proceeded to win the NBA's inaugural title and four out of the first five NBA championships. Center George Mikan was the Lakers' main weapon and the game's premier big man of that early era, but the mastermind behind the Lakers was John Kundla, a Minneapolis High School and University of Minnesota graduate. "He was a great coach, one who really understood the players," said Mikan of Kundla. "John wasn't a screamer and was very mild-mannered, but he'd let loose when we deserved it, and usually I was the first one he bawled out. The message he sent was that no one on the team was above criticism."

hough the Lakers were a successful bunch through 12 full seasons, owners of the franchise decided to relocate the Lakers to Los Angeles, California, in 1960, leaving Minnesota without a team. Minnesota had brief dalliances with pro basketball in the late 1960s. In 1967 another pro hoops league, the American Basketball Association (ABA), gave the state a team called the Minnesota Muskies, but the team relocated to Miami, Florida, after just a single season before hosting another

ABA team called the Pipers, which moved from Pittsburgh to Minnesota for only the 1968–69 season. Twenty long years later, when the NBA granted Minnesota a new team to begin play in 1989, it seemed only natural to name the franchise after one of the state's best-known predators, creatures that outdoor enthusiasts can sometimes hear howling through the state's northern forests: the Timberwolves.

The first Wolves were mostly players that other franchises left unprotected in a league-wide expansion draft, and team officials knew they needed a coach who could squeeze the maximum amount of effort out of some mediocre talent. The Timberwolves found their guy in Bill Musselman, a former University of Minnesota coach known for his ability to motivate players. "It's great to be here," Musselman said in his typically gruff style. "Now let's build a winner."

Although guard Sidney Lowe, swingman Tony Campbell, and forwards Sam Mitchell and Brad Lohaus shared their coach's affinity for hard work, physical play, and stubborn defense, victories were scarce for Minnesota in 1989–90, and the team finished 22–60 while playing in the cavernous Hubert H. Humphrey Metrodome. Fans showed their enthusiasm nonetheless, setting an NBA season attendance record with an incredible total of 1,072,572 fans filling the Dome's seats.

The next season, the Wolves moved into Minneapolis's brand-new Target Center, and young point guard Jerome "Pooh" Richardson helped Minnesota improve to 29–53. Unfortunately, the team faltered again the following year under new head coach Jimmy Rodgers, regressing to a miserable 15–67. The Wolves' poor record helped them secure the

J. R. RIDER

A SMALL VICTORY

During the 1993–94 season, when the Timberwolves made their annual visit to the famous Madison Square Garden in New York City to take on the Knicks, Wolves guard J. R. Rider treated Minnesota fans to a beautiful hustle play. Minnesota fans, a hardy lot, had watched their club assemble a combined 97–265 record up until that Knicks game—without so much as a whiff of the postseason—and were used to cheering plays rather than wins, because victories were so few. The Knicks featured one of the NBA's best centers at the time, Patrick Ewing, and on January 17, 1994, he was on his way to a 34-point performance as the Knicks built a double-digit lead. In the third quarter, on a Knicks fast break, Ewing filled the lane, received a pass, and launched his 7-foot and 250-pound body toward the rim, cocking his right arm to dunk the ball. Out of nowhere, the Wolves' 6-foot-5 Rider sprang up from behind Ewing to emphatically, impossibly, reject the ball. The Knicks' lead was just 74–67 after three quarters, thanks to a Rider-inspired rally, but Minnesota eventually fell, 106–94.

third overall pick in the 1992 NBA Draft. With it, they chose Christian Laettner, a 6-foot-11 center from collegiate powerhouse Duke University. The Wolves also traded for sharpshooting forward Chuck "The Rifleman" Person and point guard Micheal Williams.

Laettner and guard Isaiah "J. R." Rider, Minnesota's top pick in the 1993 NBA Draft, struggled to carry the franchise at such young ages. Rider was an explosive scorer, but he was also wildly inconsistent in both his play and behavior, which could be immature at best and criminal at worst. Laettner, meanwhile, grew frustrated by the team's woes. "The losing just

turns you numb after a while," he said. "I lost more games here in a month than I did my whole college career."

By 1994, fan attendance at Target Center had slipped. Many Minnesota fans found Laettner to be petulant, Williams injury-prone, Person one-dimensional, and Rider unreliable. Other draft picks such as centers Felton Spencer and Luc Longley failed to pan out. The ticket-buying public was forced to take solace in the team's small victories, which often consisted of a win over another struggling team, a close loss to a good team, or even a single standout play from an otherwise forgettable game.

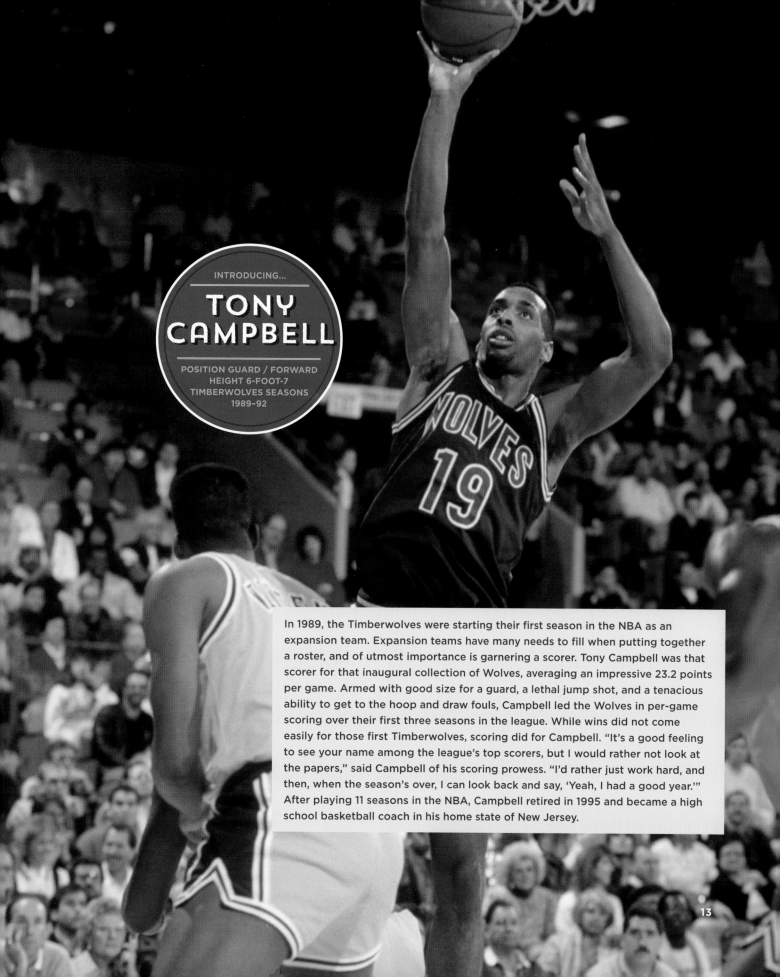

INTRODUCING...

TONY CAMPBELL

POSITION GUARD / FORWARD
HEIGHT 6-FOOT-7
TIMBERWOLVES SEASONS
1989–92

In 1989, the Timberwolves were starting their first season in the NBA as an expansion team. Expansion teams have many needs to fill when putting together a roster, and of utmost importance is garnering a scorer. Tony Campbell was that scorer for that inaugural collection of Wolves, averaging an impressive 23.2 points per game. Armed with good size for a guard, a lethal jump shot, and a tenacious ability to get to the hoop and draw fouls, Campbell led the Wolves in per-game scoring over their first three seasons in the league. While wins did not come easily for those first Timberwolves, scoring did for Campbell. "It's a good feeling to see your name among the league's top scorers, but I would rather not look at the papers," said Campbell of his scoring prowess. "I'd rather just work hard, and then, when the season's over, I can look back and say, 'Yeah, I had a good year.'" After playing 11 seasons in the NBA, Campbell retired in 1995 and became a high school basketball coach in his home state of New Jersey.

GROWLING WITH GARNETT

THE SIGNING OF KEVIN GARNETT MARKED A NEW BEGINNING FOR WOLVES BASKETBALL.

n 1994, the team was sold to Minnesota businessman Glen Taylor, and in 1995, former Boston Celtics star forward Kevin McHale assumed command of the Timberwolves' basketball operations. McHale had won three NBA championships with the Celtics, and he hoped to breathe life into the luckless Wolves. "We're officially out of excuses," McHale said. "Our fans have been patient. Now we have to give them something to get excited about."

McHale's first move was a brilliant one, selecting high school phenom Kevin Garnett with the fifth overall pick in the 1995 NBA Draft. Garnett, a versatile, 6-foot-11 forward, appeared to be the impact player the Wolves needed, but to ensure that he developed at his own pace, the Wolves hired McHale's good friend (and former University of Minnesota teammate) Phil "Flip" Saunders as the new head coach. In 1995–96, the team went an improved 26–56.

Phil "Flip" Saunders coached the Timberwolves for 10 seasons and earned a reputation as a "player's coach"—a coach with an easygoing style who gets the most out of his players through loyalty rather than sternness or intimidation. Saunders broke in with the Timberwolves after coaching his way through the Continental Basketball Association (CBA) and turning some heads, especially with the LaCrosse Catbirds, whom he coached to two championships. He joined the Wolves as head coach in 1995 just as his college buddy Kevin McHale was promoted within the organization. In 1996–97, McHale and Saunders worked together to construct the first truly competitive team in franchise history, a lineup that improved 14 wins over the year prior. Starting that season, the Timberwolves made the playoffs for eight seasons straight, reaching the Western Conference finals in 2004. Still, playoff success was hard to come by for Saunders, as evidenced by his career 17–30 postseason record in Minnesota. In 2006, Saunders and McHale had a falling-out, and Saunders was fired, taking with him a 411–326 record and his status as the only winning coach in team history.

The next year, the Timberwolves jumped to 40–42 and gave Minnesota fans their first taste of postseason basketball. Leading the way was Garnett, who replaced the departed Laettner as a team leader and averaged 17 points, 8 rebounds, and 2.1 blocked shots per game. "That kid is the future of basketball," said Houston Rockets All-Star forward Charles Barkley. "He says he's 6-foot-11, but he's a 7-footer who can run, jump, and play all three of the frontcourt positions."

But Garnett didn't carry the team alone. The 1996–97 Wolves also featured a new weapon in lightning-quick point guard Stephon Marbury, and all-around forward Tom Gugliotta netted 20.6 points per game. The young Wolves were swept from the 1997 playoffs by the veteran Rockets, but they were finally howling. The Timberwolves posted their first winning record in 1997–98, finishing 45–37 and pushing the heavily favored Seattle SuperSonics to five games before bowing out in the first round of the postseason.

Unfortunately, before the start of the next season, Minnesota's promising core was dismantled. Gugliotta left town as a free agent, and Marbury—whom many Wolves fans had envisioned feeding slick passes to Garnett for years to come—demanded a trade to the East Coast and was dealt to the New Jersey Nets. Taking their places were forward Joe Smith and veteran point guard Terrell Brandon. Garnett, Smith, and Brandon carried the team back into the playoffs in 1999, but Minnesota fell to the eventual NBA champion San Antonio Spurs in the first round.

In 1999, Minnesota drafted forward Wally Szczerbiak, who could either light it up from three-point range or slash his way to the basket. Szczerbiak and veteran swingman Malik Sealy helped the more balanced Timberwolves achieve their best record yet in 1999–2000, a 50–32 finish, yet Minnesota quickly submitted to the Portland Trail Blazers in the playoffs.

Harsher blows ensued. A few weeks after the playoff loss, Sealy was killed in a car accident. Then, the NBA ruled that Smith and the Wolves had violated league salary cap rules by secretly working out an illegal contract. NBA commissioner David Stern levied a large fine on the team, took away Minnesota's next five first-round picks in the annual NBA Draft, and forced Smith to leave the team. Despite these crushing setbacks, the Wolves made the playoffs the next three seasons only to be ushered out in the first round every time. Minnesota fans began to wonder if things would ever change.

DRAFTING A LEGEND

Armed with the fifth overall pick in the 1995 NBA Draft, the Timberwolves had quality prospects to consider. There were guard Jerry Stackhouse and forwards Joe Smith, Rasheed Wallace, and Antonio McDyess, all talented college players who would become solid pros. But then there was a question mark—a long, skinny, unproven, "high-school-aged" question mark. His name? Kevin Garnett. Minnesota vice president Kevin McHale and coach Flip Saunders at first tried to publicly over-hype Garnett before the draft in the hopes of suckering another team into selecting him so that the Wolves could pick a proven college player. But then they met Garnett. "So we went and we watched him work out," Saunders said, "and about five minutes in, I turned to McHale and said, 'We better hope he's still there at number five.'" Although no NBA team had drafted a high schooler since 1975, the Wolves pulled the trigger on Garnett. Within two years, Garnett had the Twin Cities buzzing. "I said it when he was 24," Saunders later noted, "he would go down as the most versatile player to ever play the game."

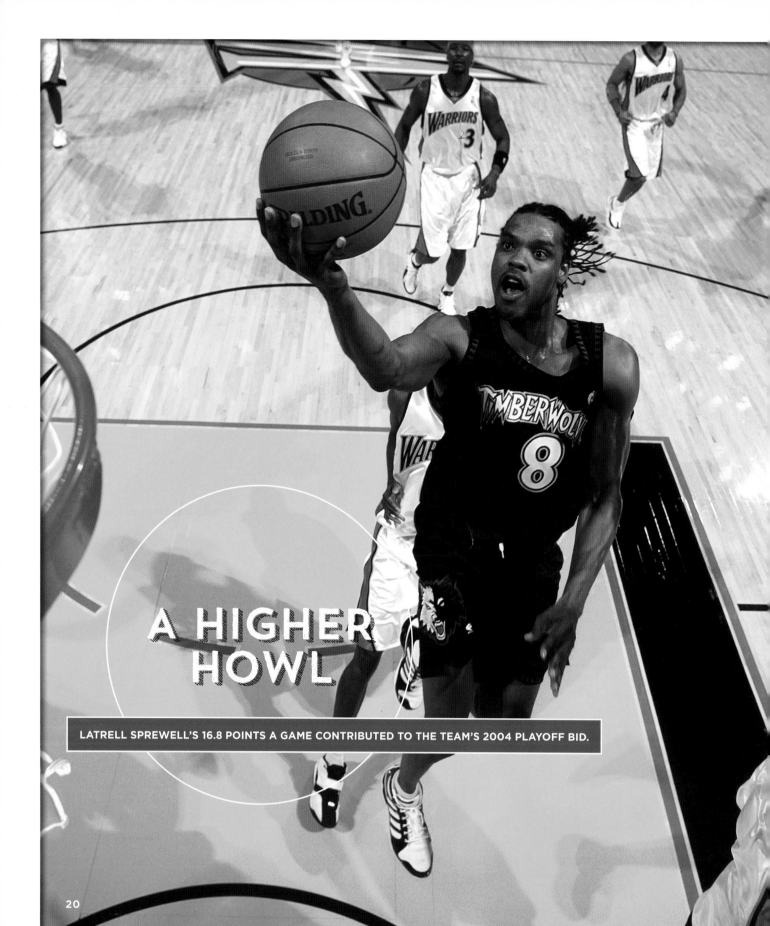

A HIGHER HOWL

LATRELL SPREWELL'S 16.8 POINTS A GAME CONTRIBUTED TO THE TEAM'S 2004 PLAYOFF BID.

Before the next season, the Wolves reshaped their roster, bringing in such players as veteran swingman Latrell Sprewell, center Michael Olowokandi, and sweet-shooting guards Fred Hoiberg and Sam Cassell. Early in the 2003–04 campaign, defensive-minded guard Trenton Hassell and sure-handed center Ervin Johnson moved into the starting lineup beside Garnett, Cassell, and Sprewell, and Minnesota was rolling. By season's end, the hungry Wolves had put together a franchise-best 58–24 record and earned the number-one seed in the Western Conference playoffs. Garnett proved to be the NBA's most versatile star, averaging 24.2 points, 13.9 rebounds, 5 assists, and 2.2 blocks per game and earning league Most Valuable Player (MVP) honors.

The Wolves made quick work of the Denver Nuggets in the first round of the postseason. Round two played out

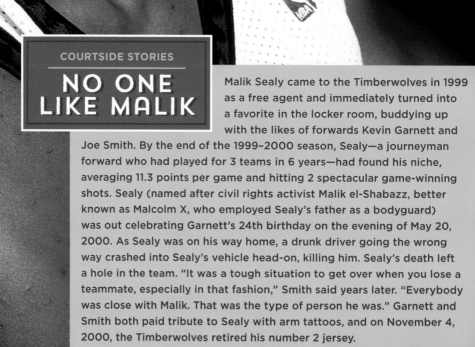

NO ONE LIKE MALIK

Malik Sealy came to the Timberwolves in 1999 as a free agent and immediately turned into a favorite in the locker room, buddying up with the likes of forwards Kevin Garnett and Joe Smith. By the end of the 1999–2000 season, Sealy—a journeyman forward who had played for 3 teams in 6 years—had found his niche, averaging 11.3 points per game and hitting 2 spectacular game-winning shots. Sealy (named after civil rights activist Malik el-Shabazz, better known as Malcolm X, who employed Sealy's father as a bodyguard) was out celebrating Garnett's 24th birthday on the evening of May 20, 2000. As Sealy was on his way home, a drunk driver going the wrong way crashed into Sealy's vehicle head-on, killing him. Sealy's death left a hole in the team. "It was a tough situation to get over when you lose a teammate, especially in that fashion," Smith said years later. "Everybody was close with Malik. That was the type of person he was." Garnett and Smith both paid tribute to Sealy with arm tattoos, and on November 4, 2000, the Timberwolves retired his number 2 jersey.

as a thrilling showdown between Minnesota and the Sacramento Kings. The series' first six games involved spectacular playoff basketball, the likes of which Minnesota fans hadn't seen since the Lakers had left town in 1960. The series went the full seven games, and Game 7 was one for the ages.

Garnett, celebrating his 28th birthday, turned in an especially clutch performance with 32 points and 21 rebounds, including 14 fourth-quarter points, in the Wolves' thrilling, 83–80 victory. "I've had some real special presents on my birthday, but nothing like this," said the star forward, who, after the game, leapt atop the scorer's table to revel with a rollicking Target Center crowd of 19,944. Saunders was among those in awe of Garnett. "I've seen him be phenomenal," Saunders said. "But in this situation, with the impact of this game, he's maybe never been better."

With the Western Conference finals up next and a ticket to the NBA Finals at stake, only the star-studded Lakers stood in the Timberwolves' way. Although the Lakers featured no fewer than four sure-fire future Hall-of-Famers in their starting lineup in Shaquille O'Neal, Kobe

THE VERSATILE TOM GUGLIOTTA PLAYED HIS BEST SEASONS IN A MINNESOTA JERSEY.

COURTSIDE STORIES

TRICKY RICKY

Since 1955, various accomplishments have been published in a bound book called *Guinness World Records*. The tome shows that the tallest man in recorded history was the 8-foot-11 Robert Wadlow. The heaviest twins ever weighed a combined 1,470 pounds and went by the family name McGuire. The largest recorded bubblegum bubble was blown to a diameter of 20 inches. The most spoons balanced on the face at one time was 17. The most balloons inflated by the nose in 3 minutes was 23. On February 24, 2012, Timberwolves rookie point guard Ricky Rubio etched his name into the Guinness record book, too, at NBA All-Star Weekend festivities in Orlando, Florida. Rubio, who had been invited by the NBA to participate in the Rising Stars game with other standout rookies and second-year players, set the record by sinking 18 shots—from behind the backboard—in 1 minute. Moments earlier, Philadelphia 76ers guard Evan Turner had set the record at 14 before Rubio hit a hot streak and, at one point, sank 16 straight. "We had a lot of fun, and I have a world record," Rubio said. "I've never had one before, and I'm excited to have one."

"EVERYBODY IS DISAPPOINTED. YOU CAN'T COME
INTO A YEAR WITH THE EXPECTATION LEVEL WE
HAD AND HAVE THE TYPE OF SEASON WE HAD."

— KEVIN McHALE ON THE 2004–05 SEASON

Bryant, Gary Payton, and Karl Malone, the Wolves seemed up to the challenge, playing the first two games to a one-one draw. But when back pain forced Cassell out of the lineup, the Timberwolves were left critically hobbled, and the Lakers won the series in six games. Still, the Wolves seemed to be on the cusp of greatness, and the Minnesota faithful eagerly awaited the next season.

nfortunately, the 2004–05 campaign turned out to be possibly the most disappointing in Timberwolves history. Cassell publicly moped after not being signed to an extended contract. Sprewell, on the other hand, was offered a 3-year, $21-million extension but turned it down, famously saying: "Why would I want to help them win a title? They're not doing anything for me. I'm at risk. I have a lot of risk here. I got my family to feed." Sprewell's comment invited ridicule in the national media, creating an unwelcome distraction for the Wolves' franchise. Sprewell had to be content with earning $14.6 million in what turned out to be his final Wolves, and NBA, season.

The poor attitude of some of the team's stars resulted in underachievement on the hardwood, and after a 25–26 start, longtime coach Flip Saunders was fired, and general manager Kevin McHale seated himself on the bench to finish the season as coach. The team ended with a winning record of 44–38 yet missed the playoffs in the highly competitive Western Conference, breaking a string of eight straight seasons of postseason play. "Everybody is disappointed," McHale said. "You can't come into a year with the expectation level we had and have the type of season we had." The Wolves resolved to make it back to championship contention, but little did they know that things were about to get worse.

KEVIN GARNETT

POSITION FORWARD
HEIGHT 6-FOOT-11
TIMBERWOLVES SEASONS
1995–2007

It's hard to put into words how valuable or essential Kevin Garnett was to the Minnesota Timberwolves franchise. Beginning in 1995, when he was drafted to wear Wolves blue and green as a gangly teen, and for the next 12 seasons, Garnett *was* the Timberwolves. "I feel like this city is mine, and I wear Minneapolis on my sleeve," Garnett once said. "I don't mind being the poster boy for the Twin Cities." With as much loyalty as Garnett showed Minnesota, it's no wonder that he became, arguably, the most beloved sports star in the history of the state. His knack for filling up the stat sheet didn't hurt, either. For 9 straight seasons, Garnett averaged more than 20 points, 10 rebounds, and 4 assists per game. As valuable as he was on offense, he was probably even better—and more dogged—at playing defense. "KG" never won a championship ring with Minnesota, and when he was traded away to the Celtics in 2007, it was ensured that he never would. The 2007–08 Celtics, powered by the Wolves' greatest star, won the NBA title.

TRADING A LEGEND

CENTER AL JEFFERSON WAS EFFECTIVE DOWN LOW AS A TOP SCORER AND REBOUNDER.

The Wolves brought in Dwane Casey as the new head coach and jettisoned Szczerbiak and other players to try to find a winning mix, but the next two seasons brought mostly losing. Even Garnett did not escape critics who said his energy level wore down in the final quarters of games and that he was too afraid to take the clutch shot.

By 2007, Wolves fans began publicly directing their ire at McHale, the so-called architect of the sputtering team. Many Wolves fans found what McHale did next unforgivable. Facing the financial burden of paying the ever-popular Garnett the NBA's highest individual player salary ($21 million per year at the time), the reality of many recent trades having gone awry, and an imminent youth movement, McHale traded Garnett to the Celtics. "I'd like to thank Minnesota for 12 years of greatness," Garnett said.

29

STEPHON MARBURY

Coming off the 1997–98 season, the Timberwolves had just recorded the first winning season in franchise history, thanks to a 45–37 record. They had a bright young coach in third-year head man Flip Saunders, budding superstars (and best friends) in 22-year-old forward Kevin Garnett and 21-year-old point guard Stephon Marbury, a hardworking All-Star in forward Tom Gugliotta, and a stable of savvy and selfless veteran leaders in forward Sam Mitchell and guards Terry Porter, Doug West, Anthony Peeler, and Micheal Williams. Too bad for Minnesota that NBA owners decided that 1998 would be a great time for a lockout. When the owners and players finally reached a new labor agreement and the smoke of the lockout finally cleared, Gugliotta, Porter, West, and Williams left via the abbreviated free agency period, and Marbury found he would never make as much money as Garnett partly because of restrictions put on lucrative player contracts and forced a trade to New Jersey. The Wolves backed into the playoffs with a 25–25 mark, and the luster was gone. "I look back on it, I'm disappointed in the way it turned out," said Gugliotta, years later. "Minnesota was a great place to play."

KEVIN GARNETT

"Minneapolis is a beautiful city. I'll always have a home there, I'll always have a special place in my heart. But I think at this point in my career, I can't do young, and I think that you need veterans to win."

The Timberwolves received five players in exchange for Garnett, but only one of them made an impact: center Al Jefferson, a 6-foot-10 offensive stalwart who relied on deft footwork and a deadly jump hook. Still, the fallout was harsh in Minnesota. The 2007–08 Timberwolves slipped farther down the NBA standings, finishing a meager 22–60, the same record as in the team's inaugural season. The franchise was literally back where it started. Garnett, meanwhile, helped turn the Celtics—who had won just 24 games the season before he arrived—into a powerhouse that won the 2008 NBA championship.

In the 2008 NBA Draft, McHale made another swap, drafting smooth-scoring guard O. J. Mayo third overall and then trading him

KEVIN McHALE

GENERAL MANAGER, COACH
TIMBERWOLVES SEASONS
AS GENERAL MANAGER
1995–2008; AS COACH
2004–05, 2008–09

Kevin McHale grew up in Hibbing, a town on Minnesota's northern Iron Range. A 6-foot-10 post player, he had an enormous wingspan and a barrel-shaped body, and he enjoyed great success collegiately at the University of Minnesota and professionally with the Boston Celtics. In 1993, McHale joined the Timberwolves' front office, eventually working his way up to vice president of basketball operations. Midway through the 2004–05 season, he also briefly took over as coach after firing longtime friend Flip Saunders, the winningest coach in franchise history. "I'm going to do the best I can," McHale said. "I'm going to try and instill some confidence in our guys and get some swagger back." The Wolves went 19–12 under McHale but missed the playoffs only a year after recording the NBA's best record. In 2007, McHale orchestrated the largest trade in team history, shipping the face of Minnesota's franchise, Kevin Garnett, to his old team, the Celtics. In 2007–08, the Celtics won the NBA championship, and the Timberwolves tied for the third-worst record in the league.

INTRODUCING...

KEVIN LOVE

POSITION FORWARD
HEIGHT 6-FOOT-10
TIMBERWOLVES SEASONS
2008-PRESENT

Rugged forward Kevin Love, with his grizzly beard and tree-trunk frame, was not always such a sure thing for NBA glory. Just ask Wolves fans who may remember palm-smacking their foreheads when the team swapped dazzling shooting guard O. J. Mayo (the third overall pick in the 2008 NBA Draft) for Love (the fifth overall pick). Luckily for those fans, Mayo faded while Love steadily improved throughout his rookie season, drawing praise from then Wolves center Al Jefferson, who said, "Kevin Love just has to have confidence. Sometimes he doesn't know how big of a beast he is, so I have to tell him." By the 2010–11 campaign, Love had figured it out to the degree that he led the NBA in rebounding with 15.2 boards per game and became only the fifth player in franchise history to be selected to the All-Star Game. In 2012, he started for the American men's Olympic basketball team, which won the gold medal in the Summer Games. "His growth will come from just expanding his game," said Wolves coach Rick Adelman of Love in 2012. "It's all there for him, and I think his Olympic experience will help him understand that."

10:31

to the Memphis Grizzlies for 6-foot-10 power forward Kevin Love, the fifth overall pick, plus forward Mike Miller. "We're really, really excited about it," said McHale. "We got the best big man in the draft, I felt, in Kevin Love, and a knock-down shooter in Mike Miller." Love had a solid rookie season, averaging 11.1 points and 9.1 rebounds per game and competing with and learning from the offensively gifted Jefferson in practice. McHale replaced Randy Wittman as coach during the season, and the Wolves seemed to be improving before Jefferson suffered a year-ending knee injury, and the team finished a lackluster 24–58.

FORWARD RYAN GOMES, ACQUIRED IN THE GARNETT TRADE, WAS NAMED CO-CAPTAIN IN 2009.

SMOOTH BALL HANDLER MIKE MILLER AVERAGED 4.5 ASSISTS PER GAME IN HIS LONE MINNESOTA SEASON.

FORWARD DERRICK WILLIAMS WAS THE WOLVES' HIGHEST DRAFT PICK YET (NO. 2 OVERALL).

RUNNING WITH RUBIO AND LOVE

KEVIN LOVE BECAME AN ALL-STAR FORCE AND A LEAGUE LEADER IN DOUBLE-DOUBLES.

JONNY FLYNN

The Timberwolves cleaned house in the summer of 2009, hiring new general manager David Kahn, who promptly overhauled the team. McHale was fired, and Kurt Rambis replaced him as the ninth head coach in team history. Numerous players, including Randy Foye and Miller, were sent packing, and Minnesota began rebuilding through the draft when Kahn curiously selected point guards Ricky Rubio of Spain and Jonny Flynn of Syracuse University with the fifth and sixth picks in the 2009 NBA Draft. Although Kahn claimed that both players would be able to play together, the move seemed to scare off Rubio, who stayed in Spain another two seasons developing his game.

Meanwhile, the routinely overwhelmed Wolves struggled mightily under Rambis, racking up the worst back-to-back seasons in franchise history. Another fresh start was made

MICHAEL BEASLEY PROVED HE COULD SCORE BIG BUT STRUGGLED WITH CONSISTENCY.

by Kahn in the summer of 2011 when he fired the coach just halfway through Rambis's four-year contract and hired Rick Adelman, one of the most respected veteran coaches in the league. "I always said one of the things we'd have to have is a great coach," said Love, who played with Adelman's son in high school in Oregon. "Now, we've got a great coach."

To add to the team's good fortunes, Rubio had finally agreed to join the Timberwolves and give Minnesota fans true hope. With the precocious Rubio showcasing magical passing and surprisingly adept defensive skills, the quickly improving Love, smooth-scoring forward Michael Beasley, and bruising center Nikola Pekovic—along with promising rookie forward Derrick Williams—raised their level of play, and the team found itself in playoff contention. "Most of the teams in town—football, baseball,

basketball, hockey—have really struggled for the last few years," said Minneapolis sportswriter Jim Souhan. "[Rubio] has made Target Center the place to be again."

Unfortunately, Minnesota's season turned sour in one instant during a March 9 game versus the Lakers. With the Wolves poised to capture the seventh playoff spot in the Western Conference as they led the Lakers 102–101 with a mere 17 seconds remaining, Lakers guard Bryant ran over Rubio on a perimeter drive, drawing the tweet of a ref's whistle. Wolves fans yelled for a charging call on Bryant, but the foul went against Rubio instead. Worse yet, Rubio remained on the floor, clutching his left knee. The Wolves lost the game, 105–102, lost Rubio for the rest of the year with torn ligaments, and lost their will to win, dropping 20 of their final 25 ballgames.

WALLY SZCZERBIAK

**POSITION FORWARD
HEIGHT 6-FOOT-7
TIMBERWOLVES SEASONS
1999–2006**

With a flick of his wrist, a swish of the net, and a pump of his fist, Wally Szczerbiak, in his years with Minnesota, won over many Timberwolves fans. A spritz of his hairspray and a flash of his toothy smile won him even more hearts. "He's the Ben Affleck or Tom Cruise of the NBA," said Gary Wichard, Szczerbiak's agent. "All the little girls love him, they want his picture, they want posters of him. And all the older women, who companies try to appeal to, like him, too." A gifted offensive player, Szczerbiak landed a job in Minnesota when the Wolves picked him sixth overall in the 1999 NBA Draft. Szczerbiak settled in as an outside complement to the inside game of forward Kevin Garnett, giving the Wolves a nice one-two punch, and in 2002, both Garnett and Szczerbiak represented Minnesota in the NBA All-Star Game. Injuries soon hampered Szczerbiak's effectiveness and hurt his already limited defensive ability. But Wolves fans will forever remember his golden shooting touch, if not just his good looks.

COURTSIDE STORIES

MUSKIE POWER

As part of a 2011–12 "throwback" promotion, the Timberwolves were selected to wear uniforms of their professional basketball-playing forefathers, the Minnesota Muskies. One of the original franchises of the American Basketball Association (ABA) in 1967–68, the Muskies were a fine team. In their lone season in the North Star State, the Muskies ran up 50 wins against only 28 losses, featured 3 players selected to the league's midseason All-Star team in Mel Daniels, Donnie Freeman, and Les "Big Game" Hunter, and had the blessings of the league's commissioner, former Minneapolis Lakers star George Mikan, who was instrumental in lobbying local investors to foot the bill to bring the Minnesota Muskies into existence. The Muskies, however, drew paltry average crowds of fewer than 3,000 fans per home game at the spacious Met Center in Bloomington. This forced the team to relocate down south the next season and become the Miami Floridians. "We just had trouble drawing people," said Dick Jonckowski, former Muskies director of public relations. "For some reason we couldn't get it off the ground."

Optimism returned to Minnesota in the off-season when the Timberwolves signed a pair of Russian-born free agents—jackknifing forward Andrei Kirilenko and crafty guard Alexey Shved—as well as capable big men Dante Cunningham and Greg Stiemsma. Love played surprisingly well with the gold-medal-winning American Olympic team in the 2012 London Games, and Rubio worked hard at rehabilitating his knee. Minnesota's 2012–13 season, then, kicked off with a high level of optimism for the first time since the Garnett Era.

ecember 15, 2012, marked the season's high point as the Wolves welcomed Rubio back into the lineup for the first time from his knee injury and downed the Mavericks 114–106 in overtime to improve to 12–9 overall. Unfortunately for Minnesota, a multitude of injuries—followed by multitude of losses—followed. Love, the team's lone reigning All-Star player, twice broke knuckle bones on his shooting hand and only played in 18 games all season, and 5 different Wolves had knee injuries that required surgery, including former All-Star guard Brandon Roy, who had un-retired and briefly given the Wolves hope at the shooting guard position.

Though the Timberwolves finished a thoroughly disappointing 31–51, there were highlights. Adelman notched his 1,000th career coaching victory, Pekovic led the team in overall scoring and rebounding totals, and Rubio's return was considered successful, as he finished second in the league in steals (2.4 per game), 10th in assists (7.3 per game), and improved his scoring average to 10.7 points per game. The

Wolves also went back to their roots during the off-season, rehiring the franchise's all-time winningest coach, Flip Saunders, in a general-manager-only role. "My goal is to help the Wolves achieve the success that we experienced during my first tenure with this organization," said Saunders.

Although slower than Saunders would have liked, success was steady in 2013–14, as the Wolves tracked their best season in a decade. Love continued to be a league standout, supported by Rubio, Pekovic, guard Kevin Martin, and forward Corey Brewer. Though talented on paper, the team lacked a deep bench and was prone to late-game collapses—which meant there was plenty of room for improvement in the future.

The Timberwolves have had two long stretches of ineptness with one period of Kevin Garnett-led excellence sandwiched between. Along the way, Minnesota basketball fans have enjoyed the riches of the game itself and the honest way men such as Sam Mitchell, Tom Gugliotta, Sam Cassell, Kevin Love, and Ricky Rubio have played it. With a new zip in their game, the Wolves are chasing an NBA title once again.

INDEX